Adaptation and Survival

Robert Snedden

www.raintreepublishers.co.uk
Visit our website to find out more information about Raintree books.

To order:
☎ Phone 0845 6044371
🖹 Fax +44 (0) 1865 312263
📠 Email myorders@raintreepublishers.co.uk

Customers from outside the UK please telephone +44 1865 312262

Raintree is an imprint of Capstone Global Library Limited, a company incorporated in England and Wales having its registered office at 7 Pilgrim Street, London, EC4V 6LB – Registered company number: 6695582

Edited by Andrew Farrow, Adrian Vigliano, and
  Diyan Leake
Designed by Victoria Allen
Picture research by Elizabeth Alexander
Illustrations by Oxford Designers & Illustrators
Originated by Capstone Global Library Ltd
Printed in China

ISBN 978 1 406 23257 8 (hardback)
15 14 13 12 11
10 9 8 7 6 5 4 3 2 1

ISBN 978 1 406 23264 6 (paperback)
16 15
10 9 8 7 6 5 4 3 2

British Library Cataloguing in Publication Data
Snedden, Robert.
  Adaptation and survival. -- (The web of life)
  578.4-dc22
A full catalogue record for this book is available from the British Library.

Acknowledgements
The author and publisher are grateful to the following for permission to reproduce copyright material: Alamy p. 35 (© GoSeeFoto); Dreamstime.com pp. 7 (© Nico Smit), 8 (© Outdoorsman), 22 (© Robert Venn); FLPA p. 23 (Mark Moffett/Minden Pictures); Getty Images p. 13 (Annie Griffiths Belt); iStockphoto pp. 29 (© MaXPdia), 38 (© ihoe); Nature Picture Library p. 26 (© Bence Mate); NHPA p. 40 (Dave Watts); Photolibrary pp. 9 (M. Varesvuo), 10 (Wayne Lynch), 11 (Doug Allan), 12 (Naftali Hilger), 14 (Arthur V Evans), 19 (M. Varesvuo), 20 (Kerstin Hinze), 21 (Alain Dragesco-Joffé), 25 (Fritz Poelking), 24 (François Gilson), 27 (Gerard Lacz), 30 (Richard Herrmann), 32 (Tim Zurowski), 41 (James Gerholdt); Shutterstock pp. 4 (© Gentoo Multimedia Ltd), 5 (© worldswildlifewonders), 6 (© Rido), 15 (© Zolran), 18 (© Maynard Case), 31 (© Studio 37), 33 (© Bobkeenan Photography), 36 (© Jon Naustdalslid), 39 (© Arto Hakola).

Cover photograph of common bottlenose dolphins (*Tursiops truncatus*) reproduced with permission of FLPA (© Jurgen & Christine Sohns).

Every effort has been made to contact copyright holders of material reproduced in this book. Any omissions will be rectified in subsequent printings if notice is given to the publisher.

Disclaimer
All the internet addresses (URLs) given in this book were valid at the time of going to press. However, due to the dynamic nature of the internet, some addresses may have changed, or sites may have changed or ceased to exist since publication. While the author and publisher regret any inconvenience this may cause readers, no responsibility for any such changes can be accepted by either the author or the publisher.

Contents

Some words appear in the text in bold, **like this**. You can find out what they mean by looking in the glossary.

Survival of the fittest

Earth is a vast tapestry of different **environments**. There are freezing **polar** regions, hot dry deserts, lush rainforests, chilly mountaintops, and windswept grasslands. The challenges for survival that each environment presents to the living things that inhabit them are many and varied – and the solutions are just as extraordinary. Those **organisms** that are best fitted to their environment are the most likely to survive – and to produce offspring that will survive, too.

Fit for life

When scientists talk about the "**fitness**" of living things, they don't mean **stamina** or muscle power. What they mean is their ability to produce offspring successfully. The fittest organisms are not necessarily the biggest and strongest; they are the ones that fit best into their environment. Over time, only the organisms best suited, or adapted, to a particular environment will survive there. This is called **natural selection**.

The emperor penguin and the quetzal (opposite) are adapted to life in very different environments. Neither bird would survive in the other's habitat. The penguin's thick layer of blubber would be ill-suited to the warm tropical forests where the quetzal is found, and the delicate quetzal could not survive the cold of Antarctica.

Adaptations

Adaptations are features of living things that are the result of natural selection. The stripes of a tiger that help to hide it as it ambushes its **prey** are an adaptation. A tiger that catches enough food to eat is more likely to produce healthy offspring than one that goes hungry because it is easily spotted by its prey. This means that over time there will be greater numbers of striped tigers than non-striped tigers. The tiger doesn't choose to be striped; the environment it lives in makes it the best way to be.

In the rest of this book we'll explore some of the many adaptations that make plants and animals fit for life in their environments.

WORD BANK

fitness capability of a living thing to survive and reproduce

natural selection process by which the living things that are best adapted to their environment

Temperature control

Staying at the right temperature is very important for life. Living things rely on the many thousands of chemical reactions that keep them alive, such as breaking down food to obtain energy. For each living thing, these reactions take place within a narrow range of temperatures. If they stray too far from this temperature range these processes begin to fail. The result can be the **organism's** death.

Animals have a number of adaptations to keep them at the right temperature. Sometimes these take the form of automatic body responses, such as sweating. Sometimes they are part of an animal's behaviour, such as finding shade.

WHAT IT MEANS FOR US

Scientists think that our naked skin and many sweat glands were adaptations to an active life in tropical heat. Our heads stayed hairy because that protects the brain from direct sunshine. Another explanation is that less body hair means fewer places for **parasites** to hide, which meant a healthier, more appealing mate.

We humans are animals too, with biological temperature control systems just like other living things. However, we are able to make changes to our **environment**. For example, we can set **thermostats** and air-conditioning in our homes and workplaces to keep ourselves comfortable, or change our clothing to suit different weather conditions.

Sweating helps the body cool down after exercise has caused a rise in temperature.

Inside and out

Mammals and birds are able to generate heat energy from the food they eat. This heat is carried around the body by the blood. They can regulate the temperature of their bodies, keeping it at the right level. Body mechanisms, such as sweating or panting, and increasing the flow of blood in the skin, help to cool the animal down.

Other animals, such as most fish, reptiles, and amphibians, have a body temperature that is always close to that of their surroundings. A reptile's body temperature increases if conditions around it are hot, and falls if they are cold. Reptiles have adaptations that prevent them from reaching dangerous temperature extremes.

The simplest of the reptile's strategies is to bask in the Sun to get warm and move to the shade to cool down. Like mammals, reptiles can expand the blood vessels in their skin, increasing the flow of blood through them. But they do this for the opposite reason. It allows the heat from the Sun to warm their blood faster. In the evening the blood vessels contract, helping to keep the warmth trapped inside the reptile's body.

Colour correction

Some lizards can adjust their temperature by changing colour. In the morning their skins are darkened because dark colours are better at absorbing heat. As the day warms up, their skin gets lighter. The lighter colour reflects some of the Sun's rays and helps to prevent the lizard from overheating.

WORD BANK
thermostat   device used to regulate temperature
parasite   animal or plant that lives on another living thing, taking food from its body

7

Keeping warm

In the world's cold places, such as the areas around the poles or in high mountain ranges, one of the biggest challenges is staying warm. One way to do this is by using some form of **insulation**.

Air is an excellent insulator as it is a very poor **conductor** of heat. Mammals such as the Arctic fox and the **polar** bear have a thick layer of fuzzy under-fur that traps tiny pockets of insulating air close to their skin. Over this is a second layer of longer and coarser guard hairs. These guard hairs keep the under-fur dry. This is important because wet fur sticks together, which means there is nowhere to trap air.

The thick fur of the Arctic fox insulates it from the cold of an Arctic winter.

Feathered comfort

Birds don't have fur but their feathers do the same air-trapping job. A layer of fluffy down feathers next to the bird's skin works just like a mammal's under-fur. In winter birds often look plump. This isn't because they've found a lot to eat – it's because they fluff up their feathers to trap more insulating air.

Cold-climate trees

Plants that grow on mountains and in the northern forests also have to be able to cope with cold conditions. **Evergreen** trees, such as conifers, are adapted to deal with cold.

As the name suggests, evergreen trees keep their leaves all year round. A leaf is a plant's food factory, using sunlight to make sugars. Because the leaves are always there, the evergreen is ready to make food whenever the Sun appears.

Conifers have needle-like leaves covered with a waxy coating that helps prevent water loss. In the winter, most of the water in the ground will be frozen, which means that the tree can't use it. The dark colour of the leaves is also better at absorbing energy from the Sun than lighter-coloured leaves.

Conifer trees are cone-shaped – which is another important adaptation. Their shape allows snow to fall more easily from their branches, leaving them undamaged.

WHAT IT MEANS FOR US

When you curl up under a down-filled duvet on a cold winter's night, you're benefiting from the heat-trapping property of feathers.

Chilly legs

Most birds have bare legs. You might see a bird keeping warm by standing on one leg while it keeps the other tucked up into its feathers. The Arctic ptarmigan (left) and the snowy owl are among the few birds that have feathers, not just on their legs, but on their feet, too.

Warm in the water

Many animals spend all or part of their lives in the water. Temperatures in the polar oceans can be near the freezing point of seawater, and yet whales, for example, can maintain a body temperature of 37 degrees Celsius (98.6 degrees Fahrenheit). To do this, they need extra protection in the form of insulation.

WHAT IT MEANS FOR US

Human swimmers don't have a layer of blubber, but they can add fat on the outside instead. For centuries, sea swimmers have smeared their bodies with goose fat (or an artificial substitute in more modern times) to provide an insulating layer over their skin.

Blubber

All mammals have a layer of fat underneath their skin. This natural insulator reduces the loss of heat to the animal's surroundings. Whales, seals, and other marine mammals have a much thicker layer of fat than land mammals. This extra-thick fat is called **blubber**. Just like body fat in land mammals, the marine mammal's blubber also acts as a store of energy.

A group of Pacific walruses flush pink as they lose excess heat from their well-insulated bodies.

Overheating

An adaptation can cause disadvantages, too in some circumstances. Blubber is so efficient at preventing heat loss that marine mammals, such as the walrus, can actually run the risk of overheating when they leave the water. Just like you do when you are hot, the walrus flushes pink as the flow of blood increases through blood vessels near the surface of the skin.

Natural antifreeze

Fish that swim in the chilly waters of the polar oceans, where the temperature can be lower than the freezing point of fish blood, produce substances called glycoproteins in their blood. These stop ice crystals from forming in their bodies. Even if the fish gets trapped in ice, its blood will not freeze.

WHAT IT MEANS FOR US

We use chemical compounds called **antifreeze** that stop the water in a car's coolant system from freezing in very cold weather. These compounds work in the same way as the glycoproteins in the blood of polar fish.

As well as having natural antifreeze, the Antarctic ice fish has transparent blood. It has no red blood cells, an adaptation to life in the oxygen-rich Antarctic waters. The fish can absorb oxygen directly through its scale-less skin.

WORD BANK

blubber layer of insulating fat found under the skin of marine mammals such as whales and seals

antifreeze substance added to water to prevent it from freezing

CASE STUDY

The camel

For animals in hot desert habitats the main problems are high daytime temperatures and lack of water. One animal that is particularly well adapted to these conditions is the camel.

Water conservation

The most obvious feature of a desert is that it is very dry. The plants and animals that live there have to be able to cope with conditions where water is scarce. For this reason, losing heat by sweating or panting would not be a good adaptation to desert life. Cooling down this way would this way mean losing precious water as well.

Water loss

The camel can't prevent some water loss from its body. However, camels can lose up to 30% of their body's water content and still survive. (Most animals will die if they lose even 15% of their body water.) When water becomes available, the camel can consume 20% of its body weight in 10 minutes!

Heat storage

Camels can store heat in their bodies. Their body temperature can rise by several degrees over the course of the day. Storing heat, rather than trying to lose it through **evaporation** conserves water. At night, when conditions are much cooler, the heat stored by the camel is lost to the air and its body temperature returns to its normal level. The camel only uses this strategy when water is scarce. If it has enough water its temperature rises by only a couple of degrees.

Keeping a cool head

Camels have a cooling system that prevents their brains from becoming overheated. As the camel breathes in through its long nose the air is cooled by evaporation. This in turn cools the blood passing through the camel's nose. The blood vessel carrying the cool blood passes close by the blood vessel carrying blood from the heart to the brain. As it does so, heat is exchanged between the two. The result is that the blood reaching the brain is cooled down. This keeps the brain several degrees cooler than the rest of the body and prevents it from being damaged by the heat.

Common confusions

The camel's hump

Camels do not store water in their humps. The hump is made mostly of fat and is used as a food reserve.

The jack rabbit has a different way of keeping cool. Its large ears act like cooling fins, radiating heat and keeping the rabbit from getting too hot.

Hibernation

Many animals live in places where food is hard to find in the harsh winters. Some animals, particularly birds, avoid the challenges of winter by **migrating** and moving to warmer places when the cold weather comes. Others escape winter by greatly reducing their body processes and **hibernating**.

Extreme survival

The **larvae** (young) of the red flat bark beetle survive through the extreme cold of winter in Alaska. No matter how cold it gets, they just don't freeze. As winter approaches, these insects produce **antifreezing** chemicals in their blood and begin to lose water from their bodies. Scientists believe that their bodies take on an almost glass-like state. In a laboratory, they have been cooled to −150 ˚C (−238 ˚F) and still survived.

Preparing for winter

An animal always needs a supply of energy to stay alive. Some animals build up a store of fat in their bodies that will provide them with energy through the long winter months. Others gather stockpiles of food that they eat during brief periods of activity. The hibernating animal also needs a safe, warm place to stay. Before it hibernates, the animal may dig a burrow or find an existing shelter, such as a hollow tree or a cave.

Adult red flat bark beetles are found under the bark of logs, where they feed on fungi.

Insulating materials

The fur of a hibernating mammal acts as **insulation** against the winter chill, but it will also find insulating materials from its **environment**, such as twigs, grass, moss, or leaves, or fur and feathers shed by other animals. It will use these materials to build a nest for extra protection. Soil is another good insulator, and helps to keep a burrow warm.

Into hibernation

A hibernating animal tucks itself up into a ball. This reduces its surface area and helps to prevent heat loss. The animal's heart rate drops to a few beats per minute and its breathing becomes slow and almost undetectable. The digestive system stops working almost completely. All of this means that the animal is using much less energy than it would need normally. A hibernating bat uses 99 per cent less energy than it does when fully active.

Common confusions

"Hibernating" bears

Bears are not true hibernators. In their winter dens their temperature drops just a few degrees below its normal level. They become very sleepy, but they can quickly become alert again if disturbed. Female bears even give birth to their cubs during the winter, showing that their bodies are very much still active.

WHAT IT MEANS FOR US

People have known for centuries that natural materials are good for insulation. Wool, plant fibres, and wood chips have all been used in the walls and roofs of people's homes. These materials are poor **conductors** and help to prevent the transfer of heat between our homes and the environment. This keeps them warm in winter as well as cool in summer.

A hibernating bat uses just one hundredth of the energy it uses when it is active.

The Arctic ground squirrel

The Arctic ground squirrel lives in the forests and grasslands of the north. It is found right around the world, from Siberia to northern Canada. Winter in these habitats brings very cold temperatures. The ground squirrel survives by **hibernating**.

The squirrel's year

The Arctic ground squirrel is a burrowing animal. Its long round body, stubby legs, and sharp claws are all adaptations to a life spent partly underground. The squirrels live in colonies made up of several burrows. There may be up to 50 entrances into the colony, giving a squirrel out in the open a chance to dive for cover if a **predator** approaches.

The squirrels are active from around the end of April until early October. The adult males are usually the first to emerge from hibernation, digging their way up through the snow to the surface. The females give birth to litters of 5 to 10 pups in June.

The young develop quickly. By late summer they will have left the burrows where they were born and begun to dig burrows of their own. This rapid development is another adaptation to the squirrel's **environment**, where every opportunity has to be taken to stock up on food during the short summer.

The adults are ready to hibernate by late August. The young squirrels take longer to build up a store of fat and may be active until late September.

Shaking and shivering

Every two or three weeks, the squirrel begins to shake and shiver. It will do this for 12 to 15 hours, warming itself back up to normal body temperature. After it stops shivering, its temperature begins to fall back below zero again. Scientists are not sure why the squirrel does this. It takes a lot of energy to warm up in this way – another reason why it is essential that the squirrel has a good store of fat before hibernating.

Supercool squirrel

The ground squirrel will spend between seven and eight months in hibernation. Researchers have discovered that the squirrel's body temperature falls to the lowest ever measured in a mammal. It actually falls a few degrees below freezing – a condition called supercooling. The water in squirrel's body doesn't freeze because there is nothing for ice crystals to form around. If ice did form, the squirrel would die.

The ground squirrel eats to gain weight.
It also stores extra food and lines its
burrow with grass and hair.

The baby ground squirrels
leave the burrow
in mid-summer.

The ground squirrel's body
temperature falls as it becomes
less active. Hibernation begins.

Females have
their young less
than one month
after mating.

Deep
hibernation.

Male
and female
ground
squirrels mate
in May.

The squirrel
awakes from
time to time,
to eat some
food.

August
July
September
June
October
May
November
April
December
March
January
February

The ground squirrels awake fully in the spring.

Defence and attack

All animals need to find food. Some eat plants, some eat other animals, and some, such as rats and humans, have a mixed diet. In order to survive, plants and animals need to avoid being eaten.

There are many strategies for avoiding being eaten – for example:

○ having thorns or poisonous leaves protects plants from grazing animals;

○ being part of a herd, like zebras, gives safety in numbers;

○ being able to run swiftly, like an antelope, is a good way to avoid being caught;

○ being big and powerful, like a water buffalo, discourages **predators**

○ ganging up to mob a predator helps protect smaller animals, such as a flock of birds seeing off a hawk.

A large African water buffalo can weigh 900 kg (nearly 2,000 lbs.) and stand 1.7 m (5 ft. 6 in.) high at the shoulder – big enough to deter most predators.

Predator and prey

The relationship between predators and **prey** is a very important one in nature. A successful predator is adapted to catch and kill, while its prey must be adapted to survive.

Bats versus moths

Bats and moths are both **nocturnal** animals. Bats hunt many insects, including moths, using the echoes from high-pitched clicking sounds to find them in the dark. (There is more about how bats use sounds to "see" in the dark on page 37).

Some moths quickly change course when they hear the bats' clicks – like fighter pilots taking evasive manoeuvres. They can even make clicks of their own in an attempt to confuse the bat. The moths can tell by the speed of the clicks whether the bat has just located them or whether it is moving in for the kill. These defensive adaptations have come about as a result of the bat's hunting strategy.

In a counter strategy, some bats have been discovered to use clicks that are beyond the moths' hearing range. Some even reduce the volume of their clicks as they get closer to their prey, like a bomber going into stealth mode as it nears its target.

Evolutionary arms race

Scientists sometimes talk about an "arms race" between predator and prey. **Natural selection** results in the predator having adaptations that help it catch its prey. The prey had adaptations that help it escape. If the predator develops an adaptation that makes it more successful, natural selection puts pressure on the prey species to adapt if it is to survive. The two species gradually change and **evolve** because of the pressures they put on each other.

Smaller birds can work together to drive off a larger predator. This behaviour is called mobbing.

Camouflage and mimicry

Many animals are protected by camouflage. Some insects have colourings and markings that help them to blend into the background. Others, such as hover flies, mimic bees and wasps. Camouflage markings also help a predator to stay hidden as it waits to ambush its prey.

Where's that bug?

There are insects that blend so well into their surroundings that they are extremely difficult to spot. There are some caterpillars that look just like twigs, and others that resemble bird droppings. Stick insects and leaf insects can look just like the plant parts they are named for.

Moths are among the masters of insect camouflage. This is a vital adaptation for an insect that is active at night but rests during the daylight hours, when it might easily be spotted and eaten by a passing bird. For example, both the lappet and the camo moth's markings disguise them so that they look like just another leaf in a leaf pile.

Common confusions

Mimicry or camouflage?

Mimicry is when one animal resembles another, such as a harmless snake having the same markings as a venomous one. Camouflage is where an animal uses colour and markings to resemble an object like a twig, or to blend into the background.

Can you spot the lappet moth clinging to the branch in this photograph?

Sitting tight

In most birds species, it is generally the female that looks after the eggs in the nest. Bright colours would be likely to draw the attention of a predator, so female birds are often more drably coloured than the showier males. This helps the females stay hidden when sitting on the nest. Newly hatched chicks are drab-coloured like their mother, for the same reason.

Mimicry

Mimicry can be a very successful anti-predator adaptation. In one type of mimicry, a harmless animal resembles one that isn't so harmless. For example, the king snake, which is harmless, has markings that are very similar to those of the **venomous** coral snake. A predator cannot tell the difference, and so it leaves the king snake alone.

The ground-nesting Egyptian nightjar is well camouflaged by its brown plumage.

WORD BANK

venomous being able to inject poison into another living thing, through a bite or a sting

Plant defences

Unlike animals, plants cannot run from danger and must protect themselves in other ways. Some plants have obvious defences, such as thorns and prickly leaves; others are not so easy to see.

Some plants can lose large pieces of themselves and still survive and re-grow. For example, grasses grow up from the base of their leaves, down near ground level where it is hard for animals to nibble them. As long as some part of the leaf remains uneaten, the grass can grow back.

Sharp deterrents

Thorns, spines, and prickles are common plant defences. All three do a similar job, but they are actually different adaptations. Spines, such as those on a cactus, are specialized leaves that have become tough and pointed. Thorns, found on plants like the hawthorn, are short stems with a sharp point. Prickles are attached to the surface of a plant stem and break off easily. The thorns on a rose are actually prickles.

Chemical warfare

Many plants use a range of chemical weapons to protect themselves. For instance, the fine hairs on the leaves of the stinging nettle contain irritating chemicals – an example you may have come across! Some plant chemical defences interfere with an insect's digestive system, so it starves to death. Others mimic insect alarm scents so that the insects flee, thinking there is predator nearby. Some plants actually produce chemicals that attract insect predators to the scene so they can attack the plant-eaters.

The foxglove produces poisonous chemicals that deter insects from eating it. These chemicals are dangerous for humans, too.

Working together

Some plants recruit their own private army of protectors. The macaranga tree grows in the tropical forests of Asia, Africa, and Australia. It has hollow stems that make good nesting places for ants. The tree also provides food for the ants. In return, the ants protect the tree by fighting off other plant-eating insects.

The partnership between the ants and the tree is of benefit to both – the ants get food and shelter and the tree gets protection from pests.

WHAT IT MEANS FOR US

Many of the wild ancestors of the plants we eat, such as lettuce, make bitter-tasting chemicals that discourage insects and other pests from eating them. Because we don't like bitter tastes either, plant breeders have produced plants for us to eat that don't taste so bad. Unfortunately, our garden salad plants now taste good to the pests, too!

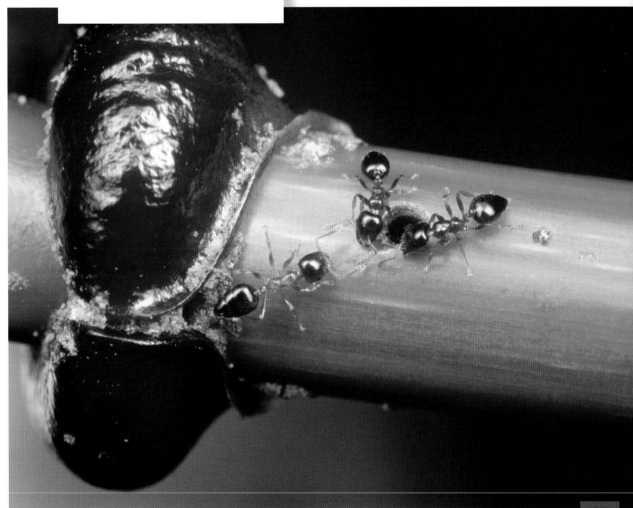

Catching and killing

Predators are adapted to catch and kill their prey. Predatory birds, such as eagles, are equipped with keen eyesight, and sharp claws and beaks. Predatory mammals have specialized teeth, such as sharp, blade-like incisors and pointed canines, to hold and kill their prey. Some predators, such as lions, wild dogs, and wolves, work in teams to hunt prey.

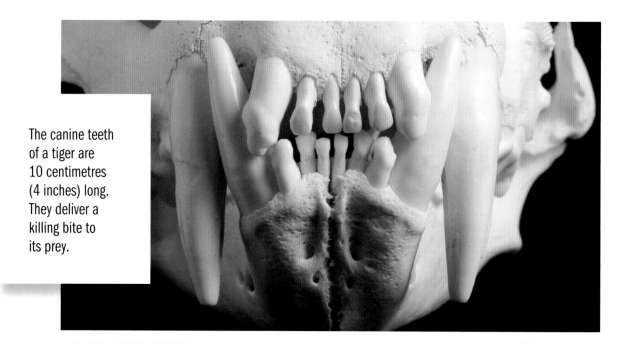

The canine teeth of a tiger are 10 centimetres (4 inches) long. They deliver a killing bite to its prey.

Common confusions

Top predators

We often think that predators are always found at the top of a food chain, but some predators get eaten, too. For example, a bird that is a predator of insects may in turn be hunted by a hawk. Predators that are not hunted by any other animals are called top predators. Sometimes a top predator can be a herbivore (plant eater), too. For example, bears will eat berries and other plant material if nothing else is available.

Swift killers

Many predators rely on a swift attack to catch their prey. The cheetah's flexible joints and spine, combined with its powerful leg muscles and large lungs, make it the speediest hunter on land. The cheetah can reach speeds of 100 kilometres (62 miles) per hour in just 3 seconds, covering 7 metres (23 feet) in a single stride. The downside is that this effort can only be sustained for around 20 seconds. The cheetah will only attack if it is very sure of making a kill.

Air-to-water hunter

The osprey is a large **bird of prey** that is specialized to catch fish. It can be found in both marine and freshwater **environments** where fish swim near the surface of clear waters. The osprey soars up to 70 metres (230 feet) above the water, searching out its prey with its keen eyes.

Its target selected, the osprey folds its wings and plunges towards the water at great speed. At the last second, it thrusts its sharp **talons** forward to grab the fish. The speed of its dive may take it a metre below the surface, so its nostrils are adapted to close, preventing water getting into its nose. Short spines on the underside of its toes help the osprey grip its slippery catch as it flies back to its perch.

The osprey is superbly adapted for scooping fish from the water.

On the tip of its tongue

Frogs and salamanders have highly adapted tongues that they use to snare their prey. A frog's tongue is attached to the front of its mouth (yours is attached at the back) and lies folded over inside. If the frog sees anything that looks good to eat, it can flip its tongue out in a fraction of a second. A sticky tip on the tongue captures the prey and pulls it back into the frog's waiting mouth.

On the move

Animals have an extraordinary number of ways of getting from one place to another. These forms of **locomotion** include walking, jumping, swimming, flying, wriggling, and crawling.

Life without legs

Snakes have become adapted to a life without legs. Their long, muscular bodies can move almost silently over the ground as they hunt for **prey**, pursuing it into narrow spaces.

Snakes have four different ways of getting around. Most move by using their muscles to send waves of movement from their heads to their tails. The tail pushes against the ground and propels the snake forward. This typical winding motion is called serpentine movement.

Some snakes pull up their tails and bunch themselves up like coiled springs. Then they thrust their heads forward as they straighten out their bodies. Big snakes grip the ground with special belly scales, pulling their bodies along in a caterpillar like motion.

Desert snakes are adapted to life on hot, loose, sandy surfaces. They move by swinging their bodies forward in loops, a motion called sidewinding. The snake's body only touches the surface in two or three places, helping to prevent it from slipping.

The basilisk lizard can escape danger by running across the surface of the water. Its paddle-like feet keep it from sinking, as long as it runs fast enough.

Through the trees

Many mammals are at home in trees. The sharp claws and flexible legs of squirrels are adaptations for running up and down trees. They have keen-sighted, forward-facing eyes that allow precise judgement for leaping from branch to branch. Apes, such as gibbons, swing effortlessly through the treetops on their long arms, or use their arms to balance as they run nimbly over the branches.

Common confusions

Flexible backbone

Snakes are not overgrown worms; they are reptiles and are related to lizards. This means that, just like lizards, snakes have backbones. A snake's backbone is very flexible, allowing it to move as it does.

A gibbon swings effortlessly through the trees. This type of arm-swinging movement is called brachiation.

Walking, running, and jumping

Many animals, such as bears, mice, and humans, walk on the flats of their feet. This adaptation gives stability. Other animals that rely on swift movements, either to catch or to escape being caught, move on tiptoe – an adaptation that greatly increases the length of their stride.

Ready to run

Mammals adapted for running move on what we would think of as their fingers and toes. A dog or cat's wrists and heels never touch the ground as it moves along. Thick pads behind the animal's claws give it extra grip and protection from hard surfaces.

Some mammals go a step further. They don't even have all of their toes on the ground. Hoofed animals, such as deer, only have two toes on the ground, and a horse only has one. The foot of a horse is highly adapted for running. What appears to be a horse's foot is just a single toe and its hoof is an adapted toenail. The hooves of deer and horses have to be tough to support the weight of the animal.

Running on tiptoe doesn't just increase the length of stride. Raising the toes and ankles up off the ground also means that more joints can be used in moving the leg forward. This means that the rate of stride can be increased, adding to the speed that the animal can move forward.

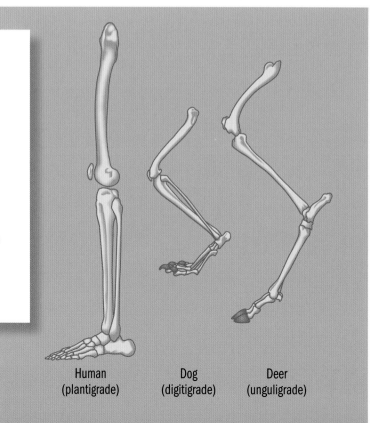

Mammals have different ways of standing, depending on how the bones of their feet touch the ground. Each has its advantages: plantigrade (flat-footed) gives stability and unguligrade (on tiptoe) gives speed. Digitigrade mammals have both speed and power and are often predators.

Human
(plantigrade)

Dog
(digitigrade)

Deer
(unguligrade)

Kangaroo hop

Some animals jump rather than walk or run. Kangaroo hops are a very efficient way of getting around. The kangaroo has large elastic **tendons** in its hind legs that store energy and propel it forward, rather than relying entirely on muscle power. A kangaroo can cover 6 metres (20 feet) in a single hop; its large tail helps it to stay balanced as it jumps. This adaptation allows the kangaroo to cover large distances in search of food, while using the minimum of energy. A kangaroo is so highly adapted for hopping that it cannot actually walk.

Swimming

The world's rivers and ocean are full of living things that are adapted to moving through the water. Some animals, such as jellyfish, can propel themselves up and down, but mostly they simply float on the ocean currents. The advantage of this is that the animal uses no energy in getting from one place to another. The disadvantage, of course, is that it has little choice of where to go. Other animals are more active in getting from place to place.

Jet propulsion and fin power

Octopuses, cuttlefish, and squid can move by jet propulsion, sucking in water and then blasting it back out again. This is a very energy-hungry way of getting around. However, it can provide a sudden burst of high speed to take the animal out of danger, or to help it catch its prey. Most of the time these animals use their fins, and in the case of octopuses their arms, to move around.

The muscle power of a fish propelling its streamlined body through the water is a much more efficient way of getting around. A fish's shape isn't its only adaptation for moving swiftly through the water. Its skin produces a sort of slime that makes the water flow more smoothly over it, cutting down on drag.

The streamlined body and powerful muscles of the bluefin tuna enable it to move swiftly through the water.

Muscle makes up to four-fifths of the body weight of some fish. To move quickly, a fish uses the big muscles along its side. These bend the fish's body from side to side in an S-shape, pushing its tail against the water to provide the thrust that moves it forward.

Swim bladder

Most fish have a sort of gas-filled bag inside them called a swim bladder. By adjusting the amount of gas in the swim bladder, the fish can change its **buoyancy** and so move up and down in the water. More gas in the swim bladder makes the fish rise, and less makes it sink.

WHAT IT MEANS FOR US
A submarine uses the same principle as a fish's swim bladder to dive and surface. Instead of a swim bladder, the submarine has buoyancy tanks. The tanks are filled with water to make the submarine dive. To make it surface again, the water is pumped out and the tanks are filled with air.

A school of dolphins leaps from the water. This type of movement, called porpoising, uses less energy than swimming through the water.

Into the air

Animals that can fly are among the most successful of all. Insects, birds, and bats have all taken to the air, each adapted in their different ways to an aerial lifestyle. Plants have also adapted to use **aerodynamic** shapes which help to disperse their seeds on air currents.

Insect air force

Insects were the first (and perhaps the most successful) of the animals to take to the air. Most species of insect can fly. Insect wings are formed from thin sheets of the same material that makes up their tough outer covering. Many insects, such as flies, don't flap their wings directly. Their wings are attached to the insect's midsection by a hinge that allows them to move. Powerful muscles inside the insect's body change its shape very rapidly, moving the wings up and down as it does so. This system allows for very rapid wing beats. A gnat can beat its wings 1,000 times a second.

Insects such as dragonflies and damselflies use muscles to move their wings directly. One set of muscles pulls the wings down, while another set raises them again.

Dragonflies are very fast and agile fliers. This, together with superb all-round vision, this makes them excellent aerial hunters.

Built to fly

Most birds are capable of flying and they have a number of adaptations that allow them to do this. Instead of front legs, birds have wings. They also have powerful breast muscles, a large heart and lungs, and lightweight bones.

Getting into the air takes sheer muscle power. The bird uses its big breast muscles to launch itself upwards with a strong down-stroke of its wings. The heavier the bird, the more lifting power it needs to get off the ground. If possible, the bird will take off into the wind to benefit from the extra lift this gives.

Seed dispersal

Plants also make use of air currents to get from one place to another. The seeds of plants such as foxgloves and orchids are so tiny that they can be blown long distances by the wind. Other plants, such as the dandelion, have developed feathery parachutes that help to keep the seeds aloft. Maple and sycamore trees have seeds with wing shapes. These spin through the air as they fall so that they land further away from the parent tree. That way the seedlings won't compete with the parent tree for light and water.

Light as a feather

To keep their weight down, birds have hollow bones that are much lighter than the bones of other animals. The skeletons of some birds can actually weigh less than their feathers.

The wing-like shape of the sycamore seed makes it spin through the air, carrying it away from the parent tree.

Senses

Seeing

The sense of sight is a powerful adaptation that has been part of the animal kingdom for hundreds of millions of years. The advantages of keen vision to help spot danger (or a possible meal) at a distance are obvious.

Field of vision

How much an animal can see at any one time without moving its head is called its **field of vision**. The eyes of **prey** animals are often placed far back on the sides of their heads, giving them a good all-round field of vision. The eyes of **predators** are more likely to be placed at the front of their heads. This allows them to judge distances accurately so they know how far away their prey is. A simple experiment will show you how this works.

If you cover first one eye and then the other, you will see that each eye shows you a slightly different view of the world. By combining these different pictures your brain can judge the distances between objects. This is called **binocular vision**.

Predators and prey have different fields of vision. Prey animals, such as the duck, generally have eyes positioned to the sides and top of the head. This gives them a wide field of view, allowing them to spot attacks from above, to the side and behind. A predator, such as an owl, has forward-facing eyes that see best in the downward and forward direction, an adaptation for hunting.

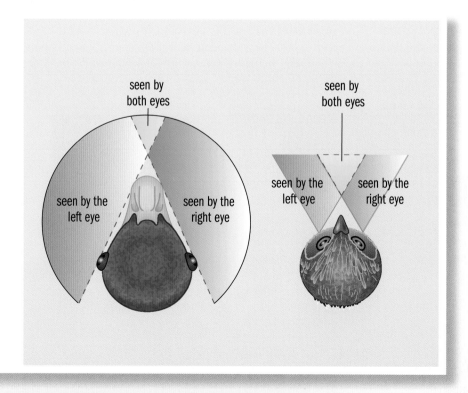

seen by both eyes

seen by the left eye

seen by the right eye

seen by both eyes

seen by the left eye

seen by the right eye

Seeing under water

The eyes of a fish are a different shape from those of land animals. For example, the part of the eye that focuses light (the lens) is oval-shaped in the human eye. But because of the way light travels through water, an oval lens doesn't work well enough to focus light properly under water. This is why things look a little blurry when you swim under water.

The lens of a fish eye is almost perfectly round, which gives fish their bug-eyed look. A round-shaped lens bends light more effectively than an oval shape, and is better for seeing under water. Because the lens can't change shape, it actually moves back and forth to allow the fish to change focus.

The anableps's eye is divided in two; the top half can see in air, and the bottom half can see under water.

Best of both worlds

A species of fish called anableps is found in the rivers of South and Central America. The anableps' eyes are unusual because they are adapted to see both in and out of the water. They can even do both at the same time. The fish can cruise just under the surface, watching for insects to eat above the surface, and at the same time keeping an eye out for danger from below. The anableps' remarkable ability may have come about through a chance change that altered the properties of part of its **retina**, the part of the eye that sends information to the brain.

WORD BANK
field of vision everything that can be seen at the same time without turning the head or moving the eyes
binocular vision vision in which both eyes are used together to build up a three-dimensional

Hearing

Being able to hear is an important adaptation that gives animals invaluable information about their surroundings. It may be possible to hear approaching danger before it can be seen, such as the rustle of a predator moving through the undergrowth. Many animals can swivel their ears towards the source of a sound, allowing them to pinpoint its position with great accuracy.

Antelope are alert to any sound that might signal the approach of a predator.

Hearing ranges

Not all animals hear the same sounds. For example, dogs can hear sounds that are too high pitched for us to hear. Snakes can detect very low-pitched sounds travelling through the ground through their bellies. Elephants also make use of low-pitched **infrasounds** to communicate. Low-pitched sounds travel further than high-pitched ones, which makes them good for communicating over long distances. Some types of whales also make use of this feature of low-pitched sounds in the ocean.

Echolocation

Some animals use sounds to build up a picture of their surroundings using something called **echolocation**. When a bat flies, it continually produces a range of sounds in **ultrasonic** frequencies that are much too high for us to hear. These ultrasounds echo back from objects around the bat and are picked up by its sensitive ears. The "sound picture" that a bat builds up is accurate enough for it to be able to hunt insects on a dark night.

Echolocation pinpoints the position of objects by bouncing sound waves from them. The sound waves can be detected by the ears of a bat or dolphin, or by the sonar on board a submarine.

Common confusions

Blind as a bat?

Bats and other animals that explore their surroundings using echolocation are not blind. They can see as well.

WHAT IT MEANS FOR US

We also make use of echolocation to keep track of objects. **Radar** is used to send out signals that bounce off objects, and are then picked up by a receiver. It is used to keep track of aircraft from the ground, by satellites to map the Earth, and by ships navigating through busy shipping lanes. **Sonar** uses sound waves, the way bats and dolphines do. Fishing boats use sonar to find shoals of fish, and submarines use it to locate obstacles and other ships at sea.

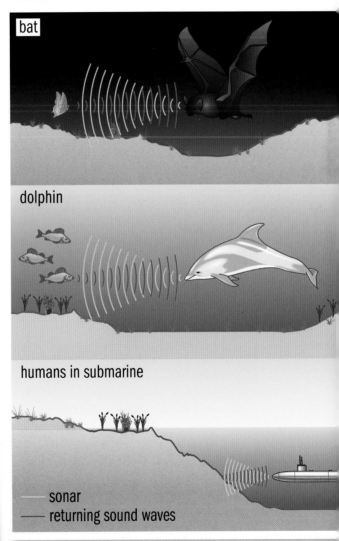

bat

dolphin

humans in submarine

—— sonar
—— returning sound waves

Smell and taste

A sense of smell is more important for some animals than others. For example, most birds have very little sense of smell. Dogs and bears, on the other hand, have a sense of smell that may be up to a million times more sensitive than that of humans.

Fish scents

Some fish have a very keen sense of smell. Sharks have been described as "swimming noses". Up to two-thirds of a shark's brain may be involved in sensing smells. Its sense of smell is powerful enough to detect a single drop of blood in a swimming pool of water.

Salmon also have an excellent sense of smell. When they become adults, they leave the rivers where they were **spawned**, to spend their lives in the ocean. When the time comes to lay their eggs, they find their way back to their home rivers. Scientists believe that they partly accomplish this feat by remembering the smell and taste of home and navigating towards it when they near their destination.

Salmon use their incredible sense of smell to guide them upriver to where they first hatched. They will even leap up waterfalls to get back home.

Bear necessities

Bears have an amazing sense of smell – perhaps the most sensitive of all animals. They use it to detect threats, mates, and meals. A polar bear can smell a seal that is a kilometre away and hidden beneath a metre of snow.

The black bear is thought to have a sense of smell that is seven times better than a bloodhound's. Bears have been known to detect the scent of a human up to 14 hours after the person has walked along a trail.

A brown bear stands tall to sniff the air. Brown bears will mark out their territories by leaving scent marks for other brown bears to find.

Common confusions

Tasting or smelling?

Tasting and smelling are very similar senses. Both rely on detecting different chemicals. The difference is that smells can be detected at a distance, but tasting is something that happens when you touch something with your tongue.

Many reptiles don't use their tongues for tasting like we do. Snakes and lizards constantly flick their tongue in and out of their mouth. If a snake's tongue is moving in and out rapidly, it is a sign that it has detected something interesting. It picks up tiny particles from the air and carries them back into the reptile's mouth. There they are deposited on to the reptile's scent detectors, which are called Jacobson's organs. It is arguable whether a reptile can smell or taste something in the air.

Sixth senses

The picture that other animals build up of the world may be quite different from the one we have. For example, we have already seen how bats use sound to "see" in the dark. There are animals that possess senses that we do not have at all.

Water sense

If you look carefully at the body of a fish you can see a line running along each side. This is called the **lateral line**. Along this line there are rows of very sensitive detectors that pick up changes in the water pressure around the fish. Tiny pores, or pits, in the fish's skin are open to the water. Along the bottom of these pores are narrow channels filled with water. Microscopic hairs in the channels react to the slightest movement of the water. The fish can use this information to tell when something is coming towards it from any direction. The lateral line detection system is one reason why you will never see a shoal of fish collide with each other.

Electrosense

Every time you use your muscles they produce tiny bursts of electricity. Some fish, particularly sharks, can detect this electricity. A hammerhead shark can find a flounder buried in the sand on the seabed by sensing the electricity its muscles produce. The hammerhead shark has electricity detectors in its unusually shaped head. As it hunts, it sweeps its head from side to side to locate its prey, like a person using a metal detector.

The duck-billed platypus is an unusual mammal, not only because it lays eggs, but also because it shares the ability to detect electricity. Sensors in the platypus's rubbery bill help it to find its prey in muddy river bottoms.

The duck-billed platypus is found in rivers in Eastern Australia. Folds of skin keep water out of its eyes and ears when it swims under water, but it is electricity in its bill that helps the platypus find its prey.

Heat-seeking snakes

Some snakes, such as pit vipers, have sensitive heat-detecting organs that can respond to changes in temperature as small as 0.003 degrees Celsius (0.0017 degrees Fahrenheit). These heat detectors are located in small pits on their heads. The snakes use this sense to track down the animals they hunt by detecting the heat from their bodies.

The pit viper's sensitive heat detectors are located in the dark pit that can be seen here just in front of its eye.

Flying compasses

Worker honeybees have a ring of iron oxide in their abdomens. This ring is tugged by the **Earth's magnetic field** – it is the same force that makes the needle of a compass move. Scientists believe that this magnetic detector helps the bees to navigate to and from their hive.

WORD BANK

Earth's magnetic field the magnetic field surrounding the Earth that makes compass needles move

Timeline of prehistoric adaptations

By studying the fossil remains of the animals that lived millions of years ago we can try to work out what sort of lives they led and what they might have looked like. Comparing them to present-day animals can help our understanding of how they could have lived. For example, if you find a fossil with fins, there's a good chance it's a fish!

The fossil records also tells us when various adaptations first appeared. The dates in this timeline are approximate, and could change as new discoveries are made.

1,000 million years ago (mya)	The first complex, multicelled lifeforms appear, though there are suggestions they could have formed much earlier.
730 mya	Animals called comb jellies appear. They are adapted to get food and oxygen from water flowing through their bodies. There are still comb jellies in the oceans today.
680 mya	The ancestors of the jellyfish appear.
630 mya	Animals appear that have a definite front and back and top and bottom for the first time. They are roughly **bisymmetrical** (have left-right symmetry), just as modern animals are. The advantage of this is that the animal can move in a definite direction, making it more efficient when finding food.
590 mya	The bisymmetrical animals split into two major groups. One will **evolve** into animals with backbones, the vertebrates; the other, into invertebrate animals that will eventually evolve into insects, spiders, crabs, and worms.
565 mya	The earliest evidence of animals moving themselves around, rather than simply drifting in the ocean.
530 mya	The first vertebrate, an animal with a backbone, appears. It may have been similar to a present day hagfish, a type of boneless fish that lives in the deep ocean. Other early vertebrates may have resembled eels.
500 mya	The first evidence that some animals are becoming adapted to spending time on land, although they would still have to return to the sea.
490 mya	The first plants begin to spread across the land, though some scientists suggest that plants might have first colonized the land about 700 million years ago.
460 mya	Fish divide into bony fish (most modern fish) and cartilaginous fish (sharks and rays).

440 mya	The bony fish divide into ray-finned fish (like the fish we have today) and lobe-finned fish. The lobe-finned fish are the ancestors of animals with limbs: the amphibians, reptiles, mammals, and birds.
400 mya	The age of the oldest known insect. The fossil was stored in a cupboard in the Natural History Museum, in London, for over 60 years before anybody realised what it was.
397 mya	The first four-legged animals evolve from the lobe-finned fish; they still have many fish characteristics. Eventually they spread out across the land, and some will evolve into the animals we know today.
385 mya	The age of the oldest known tree fossil. Trees have the strong tissues needed to grow tall and out-compete other plants for light. Forests began to spread across the Earth.
368 mya	The first amphibian appears, adapted to breathe in and out of the water.
310 mya	The ancestors of the dinosaurs, modern reptiles, and birds appear, along with the "mammal-like" reptiles that will evolve into mammals.
250 mya	Most life on Earth is wiped out in a massive extinction; the survivors include the ancestors of the dinosaurs.
200 mya	The ancestors of the mammals become **endothermic**. This adaptation allows them to control their body temperature, whatever the conditions.
150 mya	The first bird, *Archaeopteryx*, appears. It is likely that its feathers were an adaptation for trapping heat, rather than for flying.
140 mya	The first flowering plants appear. Over time, flowering plants develop a number of adaptations for dispersing their seeds and are able to spread over wide areas.
70 mya	The first grasses appear. The first evidence of grasses is in small fragments found in fossilized dinosaur dung.
50 mya	Mammals begin to diversify rapidly and spread across the world.
47 mya	Early whales are around but they are not fully adapted to life in the sea and must return to the land to give birth.
6 mya	The earliest human species branch off from the rest of the apes. Within a relatively short time they adapt to walking on two legs and using their hands to make and use tools.
200,000 to 400,000 years ago	The first *Homo sapiens* (present-day humans) appear in Africa.

Glossary

aerodynamic having a streamlined shape so as to move through the air more easily

antifreeze substance added to water to prevent it from freezing

binocular vision vision in which both eyes are used together to build up a three-dimensional picture of the world

bird of prey bird that hunts and kills other animals

bisymmetrical being symmetrical from one side to the other; for example, your left-hand side is symmetrical with your right-hand side, making you bisymmetrical.

blubber layer of insulating fat found under the skin of marine mammals such as whales and seals

buoyancy tendency of an object to float in water

conductor substance that allows heat or electricity to pass through it

Earth's magnetic field the magnetic field surrounding the Earth that makes compass needles move. Earth is like a huge magnet with its north pole near the geographic North Pole and its south pole near the geographic South Pole.

echolocation ability to detect something by the time it takes an echo to bounce back from it

endothermic regulates body temperature by using heat generated from food eaten

environment surroundings within which a living thing is found, including all the other living things found there, as well as non-living things, such as the atmosphere and soil

evaporation process by which a liquid turns into a gas without boiling

evergreen plant that keeps its leaves throughout the year

evolve develop and change over time

field of vision everything that can be seen at the same time without turning the head or moving the eyes

fitness capability of a living thing to survive and reproduce

hibernate spend the winter in a resting state

infrasound sounds that are below the pitch that human ears can normally hear

insulation material used to prevent the conduction of heat or electricity

larva (plural: **larvae**) juvenile form of an insect. A maggot is a larva of a fly.

lateral line sense organs of fish used to detect pressure changes in the water

locomotion movement from one place to another

migrate move from one area to another where conditions are better

natural selection process by which the living things that are best adapted to their environment become more common than those that are not so well adapted

nocturnal active at night

organism living thing

parasite animal or plant that lives on another living thing, taking food from its body

polar around the North and South Poles of the Earth

predator animal that lives by catching and eating other animals

prey animal that is caught and eaten by a predator

radar an instrument used to detect distant objects by reflecting microwaves from them

retina the part of the eye that detects light

stamina able to keep going come what may

sonar an instrument that uses sound waves to detect objects under water

spawn when a fish or amphibian lays a mass of eggs in water

talon sharp, hooked claw found on the feet of birds of prey

tendon tough band that connects muscle to bone in the body

thermostat device used to regulate temperature

ultrasonic very high-pitched, too high for human ears to hear

venomous able to inject poison into another living thing, through a bite or sting

Find out more

Books

Adaptation (Graphic Science), Agnieszka Biskup (Raintree, 2010)

Adaptation (Life Processes), Steve Parker (Heinemann Library, 2007)

How Animals Move, Pamela Dell (Capstone, 2008)

Life in the Wild, Michael Chinery (Lorenz Books, 2011)

Nature Got There First, Phil Gates (Kingfisher, 2010)

The Science Behind Plant and Animal Survival (Macmillan Library, 2011)

Websites

www.kmuska.com/ocean/oceanx.html
An Ocean Quest: life in a coral reef, including adaptations for living in the ocean.

projectbeak.org/adaptations/start.htm
A look at some of the many adaptations of birds to their different lifestyles.

faculty.washington.edu/chudler/amaze.html
Some amazing facts about animal senses.

www.ypte.org.uk/files/ceedu17.pdf
A downloadable pdf file about how and why animals move.

DVDs

Life, narrated by David Attenborough, BBC, 2009

Planet Earth, narrated by David Attenborough, BBC, 2006

Topics to research

Alien adaptations

Imagine what shapes life might take on other planets. Think about how conditions in other worlds could be different from those on Earth. What sorts of adaptations might life need to survive in the oceans far beneath the icy surface of Jupiter's moon, Europa?

Or how about life high in the dense atmosphere of Jupiter itself, far from any solid surface? It might seem far-fetched for there to be life on Jupiter, but writers such as Arthur C. Clarke have speculated about the possibilities, and sometimes science fiction has become science fact. What do you think?

Check out these websites for some ideas:
www.solstation.com/life/eur-life.htm
channel.nationalgeographic.com/channel/extraterrestrial/ax/main_fs.html

Marine mammals

Whales and dolphins are air-breathing mammals, just as we are, but they spend all of their lives in the ocean. How have they become adapted to this watery life? Some differences between whales and land mammals are obvious, for example a whale has flippers instead of legs, to propel itself through the water, but what other differences are there? How does a whale stay warm? How does it survive diving hundreds of metres beneath the surface?

You might find some answers here:
www.thewildclassroom.com/cetaceans/adaptations.html
www.gma.org/marinemammals/adaptations.html
seagrant.uaf.edu/marine-ed/mm/fieldguide/adaptations.html

Index